THE GOD INCIDENT

Ebenezer Sikakane

THE
GOD
Incident

EBENEZER SIKAKANE

Belleville, Ontario, Canada

All Scripture quotations, unless otherwise specified, are taken from THE HOLY BIBLE, NEW INTERNATIONAL VERSION®, NIV® Copyright © 1973, 1978, 1984, 2011 by Biblica, Inc.™ Used by permission. All rights reserved worldwide. • Scriptures marked KJV are from *The Holy Bible, King James Version.* Copyright © 1977, 1984, Thomas Nelson Inc., Publishers.

ISBN: 978-1-4600-0625-2
LSI Edition: 978-1-4600-0626-9
E-book ISBN: 978-1-4600-0627-6
(E-book available from the Kindle Store, KOBO and the iBooks Store)

Cataloguing data available from Library and Archives Canada

To order additional copies, visit:
www.essencebookstore.com

Guardian Books is an imprint of *Essence Publishing,* a Christian Book Publisher dedicated to furthering the work of Christ through the written word. For more information, contact:
20 Hanna Court, Belleville, Ontario, Canada K8P 5J2
Phone: 1-800-238-6376 • Fax: (613) 962-3055
Email: info@essence-publishing.com
Web site: www.essence-publishing.com

Printed in Canada
by
Guardian
B O O K S

"For my thoughts are not your thoughts,
Neither are your ways my ways,' declares the LORD.
'As the heavens are higher than the earth,
So are my ways higher than your ways
and my thoughts higher than your thoughts'"

(Isaiah 55:8,9).

CONTENTS

Introduction 9

Photos 25

Introducing Emlinah Sanda 29

Visiting Our Two Families 35

INTRODUCTION

After the passing away of my wife of fifty-five years, it felt as if I was left in "limbo." The need for companionship was devastating. Before her departure, she had said something to me more than once and to our daughters. She encouraged me to remarry after she passed on. I was convinced of this as I knew twenty-five percent of the authors of the grieving handbook that we had studied. They were leading evangelicals. Our leader was a very young widow who had lived for only five years with her husband.

PRAYING FOR A COMPANION

I began to think and pray for a companion. I met with a counsellor who is a pastor in our church a number of times. There were a few friends who were also praying. In October 2010, I attended the third Lausanne Congress on World Evangelization held in Cape Town, South Africa. We shared a motel with a number of international representatives. Meeting two African pastors from the Democratic Republic of Congo, we introduced ourselves. In our African culture, introduction usually includes "your family." After learning about the departure of my wife, they later took the time to encourage me because "*It is not good for the man to be alone,*" they said, quoting Genesis 2:18. In the same congress, another pastor from Asia said the same thing. It is true that God's thoughts and ways are not ours. I was encouraged to pray more confidently after realizing that more people were praying with me.

We now, Emlinah and I, bow down in humility before our Almighty Father God, who, in His great love, mercy, and grace, brought us together into the unity we now enjoy with Him in whom "all things hold together" (Colossians 1:17).

A DECADE BEFORE

In the year 2002, I had attended the fortieth anniversary of African Enterprise (AE) in Pietermaritzburg, South Africa. There I met a new board member from Pretoria. A few months later, this gentleman visited Canada on AE business. Emily, my late wife, and I hosted him. He shared his vision of planning for a bigger AE anniversary in ten years, viz. the fiftieth anniversary. He thought that former AE team members living abroad like ourselves should be present even if it meant subsidising their airfares.

In the year 2011, preparations were afoot for the AE fiftieth anniversary to be held in Pietermaritzburg (PMB) where the first evangelistic mission, named Maritzburg Mission, was held in August of 1962. At that time, I had interpreted for Michael Cassidy (the founder) and directed the choir from Union Bible Institute (UBI) some nights. After this mission, I continued to work with AE on some evangelistic missions until I joined the AE team in 1970. So Michael assisted me in raising funds in the US and Canada for the big trip to the fiftieth anniversary. Meanwhile, Emily had gone Home to be with the Lord. This was an important trip in 2012—I married Emlinah.

THE COMPANION EMERGES

The Lausanne Congress of World Evangelization that I had attended in 1974 was held in Cape Town in 2010. I attended it, and on my way back, I met with my daughter and her husband at UBI, where we were accommodated for a few days. One morning, I went to the office and met the new UBI principal and vice principal for the first time. They asked me lots of questions and told me lots about their present UBI, where I had taught. I told them about what I did in Canada, especially about teaching missions at Tyndale, which interested them. Shortly after our conversation, as I was looking around the administration building, the vice principal asked me to come to the phone. Unbeknown to me, Emlinah Sanda was on the phone asking a question that the vice principal could not answer regarding missions, and she thought that I might be able to answer it because I had just told them that I had been teaching missions in Canada.

Her question and reasons: Emlinah had been asking several organizations about the 10/40 window because she wanted to pray and possibly support a missionary working in that difficult region populated by unreached peoples. She had tried to get this information for a long time. She said that in 1998 she was invited by the principal of Child Evangelism Training Institute to attend a Global Consultations of World Evangelization (GCOWE) in Pretoria, South Africa. The main theme of those consultations was to reach out to the unreached peoples in the 10/40 window. She came back with a brand-new perspective from Pretoria. She made some serious resolutions and committed herself to doing something about unreached peoples. She got so far as to promise the Lord God that after retirement she would link up with a missionary working in the 10/40 window by prayer and a little donation that she might afford.

By the way, Emlinah had come to UBI as a student for three years while I was teaching there. We had no contact thereafter for over forty years. We never met anywhere or communicated in any way during all those years. However, I remembered her vividly when the vice president mentioned her name because she had been an outstanding student. She had obtained a teacher's certificate before coming to UBI. She was a friend of Emily, who had asked her to coach our children and also taught them at Sunday school.

After answering her question, the vice principal then went on to tell me several things about her that I had not known, viz. that she had gone on to university and obtained a bachelor's degree and that she had been back to UBI as a staff member and had also gone to Columbia University College, South Carolina for a summer course. Someone wanted to nominate her to be on the board of governors of UBI, but unfortunately, she was retired—a younger member was preferable.

August 2010 was the date of her retirement, and she intensified her search among several friends and missionary organizations who should have had a good knowledge of the 10/40 window needs and challenges, but none of them gave any helpful suggestion. It was not until October 2010 that she phoned the vice principal of Union Bible Institute, who had taught her a mission module, and this brought a glimmer of hope.

It is pretty obvious that God's hand was working behind the scenes. Emlinah's phone call was made just while I was stopping at the UBI office; the vice principal gave me all the information about the progress Emlinah had made in her leadership roles as a graduate of UBI, whose motto is *"Study to show thyself approved unto God, a workman that needeth not to be ashamed, rightly dividing the word of truth"* (2 Timothy 2:15 KJV).

CONNECTION WITH CAMBODIA

Upon my arrival back in Canada, I discussed the possibility of getting her involved with the 10/40 window. I spoke to our Global Outreach Pastor at the Peoples Church. It was obvious that no particular name could be sent to her for support. We settled on encouraging her to pray just in general for missionaries working in that region. I happened to have a good chat with a Canadian gentleman who was the founder of a good ministry working in Cambodia. So in our continuing discussion with Emlinah, she was able to support and pray for missionaries working in Cambodia with her prayer group in Eastern Cape. She sent financial support to me in South African currency, which I converted to Canadian currency before forwarding it to Vancouver BC, where the Cambodian ministry is headquartered.

Correspondence increased as I began to ask her some questions that were personal and in Canada would be under the "dating" category. She could not even be suspicious of that for two reasons. First, "dating" is not done in South Africa the way it is in Canada. Second, it was unthinkable that her former professor would ever dream of a thing like marrying his former student. She thought that all the seemingly probing questions into her life after retirement might have something to do with African Enterprise's ministry in Africa because I was involved with them. I had mentioned in our correspondence that I was planning to attend AE's fiftieth anniversary in August and that I was in the process of raising support for my airfare to PMB. She was wondering if I wanted to invite her to help set up an evangelistic mission to her city, Mthatha, because to her my questions seemed to resemble those asked by mission boards to prospective candidates.

Ultimately, I took the bull by the horns and shared my heart with her. After some time, I asked the Canadian question: "Will you consider marrying me?" After waiting for about one month, I got the positive response I had been hoping for, from a retiree fourteen years my junior.

UPROOTING PROCESS BEGINS

It became clear that Emlinah was to make the move to Canada. Of this process, she says, "It was something I could have never thought of in a thousand years. Get rid of my house and all the stuff compiled up to my retirement! Get married! Move to Canada permanently! It couldn't be real. It was already towards the end of May, and my move to Canada was to be at the end of August, after the wedding ceremony to be held the same month. My brother Nelson became a great problem solver when he offered to buy all my stuff—my property, car, TV, furniture, everything—you name it! He immediately, almost miraculously provided all the cash for expenses necessary before the day of my departure. It is indeed 'no secret what God can do.'"

Preparations for the ceremony went with amazing speed within those two months. Invitations went out to family and friends, far and near. Our friends from as far back as the Union Bible Institute days were represented among the approximately two hundred people in attendance. The ceremony was held in a church that I had selected. It went very well. From there we went to a hotel park to have pictures taken. Then, from there we drove through the city called Mthatha. Emlinah's brother Nelson had gone all out without my knowledge and arranged with his friend who had an open coupe to drive us through the city escorted by municipal police cars with sirens to control traffic. The convoy of cars took us to the reception hall where the eventful day ended with great joy.

BRINGING HOME THE COMPANION

After we arrived at the decision to get married, I did not know where to start the process of getting Emlinah to come to Canada. I knew I had to sponsor her. I knew I would have to approach the Canada Immigration office. So, I went through the Yellow Pages and found "Immigration," which was a few blocks away from where I live in Etobicoke. I made my first phone call, and I followed it by walking through the main door of their building downstairs the following morning. The concierge surprised me when he said there was no immigration office there. I maintained that the Yellow Pages showed that it was in that building. He said there were only immigration lawyers there. I asked him to direct me to their receptionist. Indeed, I found them on the third floor. Their pleasant receptionist asked me if I had an appointment with someone. I said, "No, can I speak to someone?" She directed me to the lady who is apparently in charge of the immigration services.

The lady gave me a warm welcome and a comfortable chair to sit in, which is unusual when you visit some of these big impersonal offices where you are just a number. Cristina was the nicest petite young lady you can find. After listening attentively to me explaining my need, she carefully explained the difference between immigration lawyers and Canada Immigration. Her explanation was so clear and so practical that I left her office convinced that she was going to enable Emlinah to obtain a visitor's visa to enter Canada.

I got back home with a long list of information, documents required, and forms to fill out and return to her. I worked as hard and as fast as I could to ensure that I fully complied with the young lady's orders. I called her a good number of times when I encountered problems, and I got all the guidance I needed. In fact, I felt like I was her only client; actually, she dealt with piles of files that were neatly arranged in her office.

After the completion of the first part of the work, we had an extended time with Cristina, preparing all the documents to be sent by courier to Emlinah in South Africa. Emlinah had to fill out lots of forms and sign them before sending them by courier to the Canadian Embassy in Pretoria, South Africa. You cannot imagine the number of emails and phone calls that went on in the triangle between these offices. I breathed a deep sigh of relief when the courier confirmed arrival of the documents in Pretoria. And would you believe it, her visitor's visa was ready for pick up within the two weeks promised by Cristina the very first day I met her!

The Psalmist of old wrote, *"For this God is our God...he will be our **guide** even to the end"* (Psalm 48:14, emphasis added). From this point on, it felt like being guided by an invisible light lining up my visible ducks from one point to the next. David must have experienced something similar when he said in Psalm 23:3, *"[My Shepherd]* **guides** *me along the right paths for his name's sake"* (emphasis added).

As mentioned previously, my former supporters from Canada and the US provided my airfare to attend the AE's fiftieth anniversary held in Maritzburg. The visa was issued on May 30th, thus giving enough time for Emlinah to find a pastor to officiate at the ceremony for exchanging vows in South Africa. This meant that I was going to be in the country for the anniversary and from there drive down to the Eastern Cape for that occasion. Since I had already purchased my air ticket, our travel agent managed to get Emlinah's seats on my flights from Durban to Toronto via Amsterdam. We could not take that for granted because that was a busy summer with the Olympics in England. It was so timed that we indeed "killed two birds with one stone."

Our official wedding was held in Canada where it had to be registered. The way this happened was in absolute keeping with our cultural practice. It took place first at the bride's home and culminated in the groom's home where she had to join her new family. In the Xhosa custom, she had to burn all bridges behind. We went to the marriage office in Etobicoke, very close to our lawyer's offices, to get our marriage licence. Thereafter, we were married in our church officiated by the counselling pastor.

SPONSORSHIP

Soon after our wedding, we were back to Cristina's office for another major phase in our marriage. That was to start applying for Emlinah's Permanent Residence Visa. Cristina made new lists of documents—dozens of these to support the application. As her sponsor, I had to qualify for that role. My income tax forms were needed. The documents confirming her citizenship of South Africa were required. The proof of her friendship with our family was to be confirmed in photographs formal and informal.

In the past, a friend from Seattle had sponsored our twin sons who had entered the US on a study visa. Things of a personal nature that he had to declare surprised me. As I remembered that, comparing it to what I had, I thought I would never qualify as a sponsor. But Cristina thought I would. And I did.

APPLICATION FOR CITIZENSHIP

She sent us to the Citizenship and Immigration Canada (CIC) lawyer in the heart of the city of Toronto. This is one of probably five lawyers authorized by the government to examine prospective landed immigrants medically and submit the final report to the immigration office in the province of Alberta. Cristina sent the package to Calgary. (By the way, our papers were in Calgary when the June 2013 "Noah's" deluge hit Alberta.) That was the beginning of the usual delay in the processing of applications in busy offices. We were promised a number of months, and the flood came just over that period.

FINGERPRINTS

Canada needed to know if the applicant had ever been convicted of some criminal act. She had to send to the South African head of the police department for it. We went to the S.A. Consulate to have her fingerprints lifted and sent to South Africa. We sent the envelope via courier with the pre-paid return envelope. We requested the response before the applications were mailed to Alberta. We thought that there would be enough time to do that. A few days before the application was sent, we emailed Pretoria, but they responded by asking for our email address! Well, everything was in the courier envelope that we had sent. There was a horrible confusion. We phoned, emailed Pretoria, the courier office in Toronto, their head office in the US. That is half the story. Eventually, we continuously dialled the courier number and drew a blank each time, Finally, we answered the door. The courier messenger dumped an old-looking envelope in Emlinah's hand and literally *ran* back to catch the elevator without requesting her to sign for it! The envelope looked as if it had been sandwiched between two big parcels for days in some warehouse. This was confirmed by the signature of the head of the police department dated two weeks prior to its delivery to our home.

MEDICAL TESTS

Emlinah was referred for medical tests, and we went back and forth to numerous doctors' offices for months on end. We began to understand that the system here in Canada simply left no stone unturned. These had to be done before she was issued with OHIP, SIN and permanent residence documents. We learned that she could either be quarantined, treated, or even have her application refused. We are grateful that it did not come to that at any point.

We had just started the runaround when we unknowingly stumbled on Stonegate Community Health Centre. This health centre was mentioned by a nurse referring us to a doctor who would be closer to our home. She did not describe what it was all about and how it functioned. We found that it was an outfit that helped newcomers to Canada, and it was immensely helpful as we discovered when they welcomed Emlinah.

As a newcomer, Emlinah, who had no OHIP, had to pay for all her medical expenses. "Our Stonegate," as we fondly referred to her thereafter, took that burden off our shoulders. One example: we went to a specialist in one of the Toronto hospitals. The receptionist asked us to pay for the service. The conversation went something like this: "How are you paying for this?" As I reached for my wallet, she was pointing at the amount. Emlinah and I looked at the amount and then looked at each other in disbelief. We were totally dumfounded to the point of being left speechless! $1,000! "When Stonegate referred us to this specialist, they did not tell us about this charge." The receptionist asked, "Do you want to go back and make arrangements with them?" I said, "No, we waited too long for this appointment to cancel it. Can you call them and let them know our dilemma?" After consulting with her supervisor, she made the call while we anxiously waited. Stonegate paid the bill. Stonegate then asked Emlinah to give them her health card number just as soon as she received it. We presumed that they would be reimbursed by OHIP for the charges.

The other experience that took the breath out of us was finding a health insurance company in case she took sick before qualifying for OHIP. We took the first policy for three months, paying just under $2,000, hoping that OHIP would take effect within that time, as some people advised us it would. In fact, OHIP took much longer. So, we went to another company for three more months, paying under $1,000. Unlike the first company, which paid $200 for dental work, the second did not pay even a dime in spite of promising to pay for prescriptions. It was a "mistake," I was told by their secretary over the phone!

THE WORK PERMIT

The long-awaited work permit finally arrived. We were excited. We rushed to the Academy of Learning College on Albion Road to apply for admission for PSW training as directed by the permit document from the government. We were confronted with a problem far beyond our expectation. We were told that it would take her six months to go through the academy and that it would cost her $5,255. We could never afford it. The snag was that after spending that kind of money, she would not qualify for any employment because she is retired. There is hardly a company that could employ her. So all those we had previously approached about the possibility of employment after she received her permit seemed unwilling to employ her after completing her PSW. This is simply the bureaucratic rigmarole that you occasionally find yourself confronted with in many countries. Our son faced this when he entered Canada. He had studied in the US before moving north of the border. Several employers looked at his resume, and he was tested and received regrets in one of three things—one of which would certainly be true: 1) you are overqualified; 2) you are underqualified; 3) you lack Canadian experience.

This was not the first time that Emlinah had been confronted with a dilemma of this nature. Prior to leaving South Africa, her understanding was that when she moved to Canada her retirement support would be available to her monthly. So when she arrived in Canada, she tried to find the same bank that she dealt with in South Africa and found that it did not exist in Canada, as she was promised it would. After successfully obtaining her retirement funds here in Toronto a couple of times using an international credit card, South Africa advised her that it was terminated. She was in the category of people who were not to legally receive retirement while living abroad even though she had worked there all her life. This was all by legislation. So South Africa no longer sends the equivalent of what is here called "CPP" to all the thousands of people who left the country presumably because of apartheid.

PERMANENT RESIDENCE

Twenty months ago, as roughly estimated by Cristina when we submitted our application, an all-important phone call came to us with the message, "We are pleased to advise you that processing of your application for permanent residence has been completed." This was the greatest news indeed. It meant that Emlinah no longer needed a work permit to work in Canada. She had been trying to find something to do up to this point without success. The stumbling block that remained was that she had retired before coming to Canada. The only thing that did not accompany the good news—and which never does—was her permanent OHIP and SIN cards. We speedily drove to Cristina's office to pay the Right of Permanent Residence fee, which had increased. We also paid final Transaction Amount. We are still to be scheduled to an appointment at the Immigration Centre in Etobicoke to do the landing procedure. This is supposedly the last thing in this permanent residence "saga."

PERMANENT RESIDENCE CARD

Finally! On July 28, 2014, Emlinah received her Permanent Residence card. "Congratulations, you are now a permanent resident of Canada," declared a court official. "In eight to ten weeks you will receive your Permanent Residence card...which entitles you to receive many benefits..." and he enumerated some of them. That was the most pleasant interview ever. The relief and settled feeling it brought to her was interesting to watch. She will be receiving her permanent OHIP card, four weeks before the SIN card. She will now be able to live, work, or study anywhere in Canada. She has never found a job. She loves and enjoys volunteering.

PHOTOS

Wedding

Ebenson

Rosemary

Rose

Crown (twin)

Wiseman (twin)

KZN families

INTRODUCING
EMLINAH SANDA

Emlinah grew up in a very strict home. Her mom, Louisah, was the strictest parent. Both parents were very religious. The evening prayer was strictly kept, and everyone had to attend, dressed up appropriately. Everyone had to sing and recite both the Lord's Prayer and the Apostolic Creed. A very firm warning was given to her and her sister against falling in love because that would lead to pregnancy. And if she ever got pregnant outside marriage, she would have to "dig her own grave," (figuratively) before doing it because she would be severely punished. Emlinah took the warning very seriously. She never did it.

The mother's warning became clear when she came to know Christ in a personal way. It was then internalized when she read the Bible for herself, discovering that her body was the temple of the Holy Spirit (1 Corinthians 3:16,17). She read a small booklet entitled *Keep Yourself Pure*, which was instrumental in her deciding to give herself fully to serving the Lord and keeping herself pure. Other encouraging Scriptures like Jude v. 21, 24— *"Keep yourselves in the love of God"* and *"To him who is able to keep you from stumbling"*—helped her to cement the reality of being a single missionary, which she was all her life until retirement.

One of her highly esteemed teachers contributed significantly to this. That lady got her sarcastic message across effectively. She said to her class, "A bad boy will come to a girl and deceitfully tell her, 'I love you' instead of saying 'I hate you.' You will know their lies after they make you pregnant. They will have got you out of school to look after their baby, while they continue schooling and deceiving more girls. Such girls will remain deceived cheap 'street girls.'" The teacher's message sank deep in her heart, and she was very determined to remain a spinster. That determination changed only after her retirement when her former professor who had become a widower asked her to marry him.

Emlinah's story is interesting. When she reached her "marriageable age"—in her early teens—her father pulled her out of school, hoping that someone with enough *lobola* would marry her. Lobola is a custom whereby eleven herds of cattle are paid by the groom for his bride—not buying her.

A little diversion here: a story goes like this—a missionary lady was horrified by that custom. The very thought of selling and buying a girl for a wife was to her demeaning. She expressed this to an older African man she had befriended on the mission field. The African gently asked if the missionary might let him feel her biceps. After feeling her biceps, the African slightly shaking his head said, "A bridegroom would probably not pay even a goat as a lobola for a bride who is not strong enough to do the hard work she would be expected to do in Africa."

Emlinah resisted her dad's intentions with all her strength. She expressed neither desire nor readiness to marry. Beyond that, she committed herself to what is called *isiguqo* in Xhosa. That means a place of prayer where one prays alone daily outside the house. She did this for two years. She was asking God to change her parents so that they might allow her to go back to school. God answered her prayer, and her father granted her the privilege of continuing with her education.

She entered a teacher training college, which was her dad's choice. After graduating, she did not enter that profession because she fell sick and was hospitalized just before writing her final examinations. While lying in her hospital bed, she prayed and promised the Lord that if He healed her, she would serve Him in the mission field for the rest of her life. She was discharged from hospital much earlier than expected. This was a miracle because the illness she had was expected to keep her in hospital for months. Instead, she was discharged and she got to school in time to write exams and graduate with her class. All this had been ruled out when she was admitted.

In the midst of the conflicting interests, the promise she made to the Lord landed her at several places of ministry. She entered her first Christian ministry in Madwaleni, then served at Canzibe, Decoligny, Zithulele Mission, and finally Union Bible Institute, where she actually prepared herself for missionary work. She describes how she heard about UBI:

"A friend, who is a nurse, told me about Union Bible Institute and highly recommended it to me. Her husband, who is a pastor, graduated from UBI. She also told me about a gospel preaching lecturer there. She spoke very highly of Pastor Ebenezer Sikakane, who I had never heard of before. When I got to UBI and attended his classes, I fully understood what my friend meant. The Biblical message of the gospel was made very clear. We understood how Christ transforms the lives of those who fully yield to Him and use them as they make Him Lord. Our professor left UBI to work with an evangelistic team called African Enterprise in 1970. I never thought I would see him and my friend Emily again. I heard later when I joined the UBI staff that the whole family had moved to Canada in 1978. It was only until 2010 that I heard his voice on the phone. Surely, *God's ways are higher than ours!*"

While she was at her first ministry at Madwaleni, her dad was very unhappy and he with her brother went to fetch her because they had found her a teaching position in a neighbouring school. The teacher's salary was way higher than what the mission was paying her. Instead of returning home with them, she disappeared and spent the whole vacation at a church campsite staying with a Sunday school girl. A missionary couple provided her with all she needed for the whole time she was there. When schools re-opened after the summer vacation, the teaching position had to be given to someone else.

After a couple of years in the ministry, the Lord provided Emlinah with a teaching ministry at UBI, where she had been trained. Again her dad led a stronger delegation to bring her back home. By this time she was Matron and also lecturing on Christian Education. This delegation came from the so-called nation of Transkei and had to apply for passports and visas in order to enter another so-called nation, Kwa-Zulu Natal, which by then was a "foreign country." (This was Dr. Verwoerd's Apartheid pipe-dream in attempting to Balkanize South Africa.) The delegation demanded to meet with top leaders of the school.

The way the discussion was going, the principal of UBI was almost giving up on Emlinah's continuing to work at UBI. He was wondering where he would find someone to teach her class and carry out all her responsibilities the next day! But Emlinah confidently assured the principal that that was not about to happen. Indeed, they drove back home without her.

After teaching at UBI for nine years, Emlinah returned home to minister among children and young people. She planted over sixty Good News Clubs with the organization called Child Evangelism Fellowship. She worked on this until her retirement. Both parents had passed on by that time. This was the time she did the major part of her ministry. She saw two churches that were planted as a result of the Good News Clubs.

The relationship with her parents had healed up wonderfully prior to their departure, as well as with her brother. They had come to recognize that her calling into Christian ministry was genuine. Their reconciliation was so real that when she finally retired, her brother bought her a car, which she used as she continued to work with young people and planting clubs as a volunteer. On the home front, she was planning to build herself a house on the freehold property that she had acquired. She was going to live on her meagre pension provided by the government and an even smaller savings. She was part of a group called *Masingcwabane*, meaning "let us pool our funds together for our burials." She felt a calling to pray for missionaries with her friends as well as sharing with them out of her meagre retirement funds, possibly with her friends when they would be able to do so at some point.

CONCLUSION

The crowning experience of Emlinah's life was when she asked her dad to help organize evangelistic tent meetings on his property. This was after the experience with Lord that changed his life. Besides being a new man in the family, he had become a preaching elder in his own church. He joyfully set up the evangelistic meetings with evangelists who Emlinah had approached. The majority who attended and were mainly converted were religious residents of our community who packed the tent every night to hear the saving gospel. These many converts included Emlinah's strict mother, who openly testified right in the tent about how Jesus Christ had freed her from being religious to having a relationship with Jesus Christ Himself. Amen.

VISITING OUR TWO FAMILIES

It took us a very short time to get married forty-two years after we met. We had not met any of our families—each other's in-laws. So we thought it would be a good idea to fly back to South Africa from Canada. Our plan was to start from Eastern Cape (Emlinah's province) and move northwards to Kwa-Zulu Natal (Ebenezer's province). We were barely toying with the idea when we started sharing it. Friends were willing to finance the trip. We took the trip in November 2014. It was a super trip. We met *all* the family members from each other's spouse that we had never met before. We cannot adequately describe the joy this meant to them and to us.

The other side of the story is the challenges we faced from the day we boarded the plane in Toronto to the day we boarded our returning plane. In each case we had to return home from the Toronto airport and from the Johannesburg airport—virtually minutes before stepping into the plane. When we got to the check-in counter at Pearson airport, the officer said we could never board the plane without Emlinah's Permanent Residence card, even though we had documents proving that she did have that status. By sheer coincidence, when we arrived back at our building with all the "pile" of luggage we were carrying, our good neighbour was in the same elevator with us. We were very embarrassed when we had to explain the reason. The pile of luggage was required because we were going to be speaking in churches on our trip; as we qualified for missionary status, British Airways allowed each of us to carry three free suitcases.

Early the following morning, we were at the citizenship office to inquire about the PR card. The government office had sent it to the lawyer's office through whom the application for permanent residence had been filed. No one knew who Emlinah was because the lady who knew her had moved on to another company and the lawyer's office was in the middle of moving their offices just up the road. So, the PR card was returned to Nova Scotia!

Meanwhile we had phoned our travel agent in Vancouver BC immediately after our rejection from the check-in counter. The travel agent transferred our bookings to KLM and she was to confirm our seats if we found the PR card. We found only the promise that it would be sent to us from Pretoria and that our first *duty* upon arrival in South Africa was to call Pretoria. We did. They promised us thirty days to receive it. That suited us well because it would be ten days before flying back to Canada. It was only then that we could call our hosts with the last minutes changes to arrival time—less than twenty-four hours!

We arrived in Johannesburg after midnight, dog-tired. The Lord provided an employee of the airport who took us to our hotel room. This was after his work hours. We would never have been able to find that hotel ourselves in a thousand years. He got us something to drink; he promised to come and take us to our plane to Durban departing at 6:00 a.m. We had to be ready and dressed up for the 10:00 a.m. church service at Kwa-Mashu, a city north of Durban. That young man was the first of a string of people the Lord miraculously lined up for us.

KWA-MASHU HOLINESS UNION CHURCH

The pastor of that church was Adromat Lushaba. She was a classmate of Emlinah, and they were in my class together at Union Bible Institute. She has a good vibrant congregation. She has appointed a number of pastors in their church plants. There were people from those church plants who had come to be with us. We both had time to share in that time of worship. The worship time was very uplifting. We stayed with her a couple of days looking around. Her son and his wife, who is a pharmacist, helped us a great deal in contacting Pretoria for Emlinah's PR card. They became the point of contact for us, and they were going to have it sent to their address. Adromat accompanied us with her son-in-law, who drove us to Mthatha, which is Emlinah's home. It was a five-hour drive from Kwa-Mashu to Eastern Cape. It was a beautiful Garden Route drive, partially along the Indian Ocean. The beauty of South Africa was absolutely stunning. No wonder we call South Africa the Land of Sunshine.

CITY OF MTHATHA

Emlinah's niece, Melezwa, working as a physician in King Williams Town, welcomed us in Mthatha. Melezwa is the youngest of eight children born to Emlinah's sister. She was given to Emlinah, her spinster aunt, to live with her because Emlinah had asked her sister for her and she brought her up through school until she graduated from medical school. Melezwa is now a practitioner in a large city called Port Elizabeth.

Melezwa placed us in a beautiful guest house close to where she and her husband, Onke, live. It was an ideal location for us. The dozens of people who came to see us met us in that facility, which had a large lounge equipped with refreshments. The first group that came was led by the pastor who officiated at our wedding. Some families asked us to go to a restaurant in that neighbourhood. There were some professionals who told stories dating back to when Emlinah taught them as teenagers in her Good News Clubs. One testimony that amazed us was that of a surgeon who clearly remembered the day he gave his life to Christ when he was five or six years old. He and his physician wife were expecting their second baby.

KWA-ZULU NATAL

From Mthatha, Melezwa and her husband drove us to Pietermaritzburg, the capital of Kwa-Zulu Natal Province. This is the province where all the Sikakanes had lived. Apartheid had scattered them from there—the south to the north borders of the province. Pietermaritzburg is where the Union Bible Institute is. I studied and taught there, meeting Emlinah when she was a student. She also taught there many years later.

We stayed with our nephew, Shadrack, whose mother is my only surviving sister. Shadrack provided accommodation and transportation to the relatives who met Emlinah for the first time. His mother was very excited to receive delayed customary wedding gifts that Emlinah brought her. She was very healthy, even though she is older than me, her baby brother.

SWEETWATERS HOLINESS UNION CHURCH

Shadrack drove us to Sweetwaters, where we stayed with Dumisile Mbanjwa, who trained at the same teacher training college as I did—Evangelical Teacher Training College. She was the matron at UBI when Emlinah was a student there. Later, Emlinah became the matron. Dumie was a lecturer in the ladies' department and is now one of the ordained pastors of the Sweetwaters Holiness Union Church—still involved in the ministry after her retirement. We stayed with her and enjoyed the wonderful time of fellowship the day we spoke at her church, which is situated almost across the road from UBI.

This was a very familiar place to both of us because of our association with UBI as well as this church. Many people were new to us because we had taught at UBI and ministered as guests in the church over forty years before. Now the majority of adults in the church were young people or unborn then, as far as we could see. The wonderful Christian who led the worship surprised Emlinah when he told her that he was in her Sunday school class together with five Sikakane children. He had recently retired as a cabinet minister in President Zuma's government even though he still remains a member of an important government committee.

CITY OF EMPANGENI

This city is in the heart of Kwa-Zulu Natal. My great-grandson, Israel, picked us up and drove us to his home in Empangeni. He is the principal of a high school and was ordained as a pastor while we were in that city, as will be mentioned later on. This trip was a drive along the Indian

Ocean heading north. It was the continuation of the Garden Route we enjoyed driving to the Eastern Cape. Changes and growth developments that have taken place can hardly be exaggerated. A number of people we know in this city have purchased beautiful homes that were built by whites who lived there during the days of Apartheid. The city is multiracial now.

Israel assisted us a great deal in visiting friends and family, introducing Emlinah to them. One of these was Brother Esau and his wife, Lillian Nxele, who spent some weeks visiting us to attend my classes at UBI. He had planted several Baptist churches around Kwa-Zulu Natal before he retired from the many businesses he owned and personally managed. He had built a house and bought a car for us. We paid him back fully over several years.

We then visited my late wife's sister, Ettie. She was spending some time with her daughter, Phyllis, recuperating. Phyllis had stayed with us at UBI, schooling from high to graduating as a nurse. She met and married my former student at UBI, and he planted a big church near Empangeni. He has retired now. My sister-in-law Ettie was extremely happy to meet Emlinah. She asked us not to lose contact with each other. We have been calling her since.

We were privileged to speak at Sikhawini Baptist Church, whose pastor is our great-grandson. It was a good-sized energetic congregation. Our friend Esau had tried to encourage Israel to go and study the Bible at our institution so that the Sikakane name would be retained there (not a good reason). He could lecture there because his gifts seem to be in the area of preaching and teaching. My friend must be happy now that Israel is both a pastor as well as a school teacher, doing such a good job.

CITY OF VRYHEID

A few days after arriving at Empangeni, the senior pastor of Israel's denomination came to meet us. He brought an invitation from the president to me to speak at the national conference to be held in Vryheid. I agreed to do so. I did not realize how big that event was until Israel gave some details. He drove us there—that was a five-hour drive. We spent one night in a very good bed and breakfast hotel.

On our way there, we stopped at a college that used to be Evangelical Teacher Training College (ETTC). It was built too close to the white, very Afrikaans city, so it had to be closed under the Apartheid madness. It was only after the dismantling of the system that it was re-opened as a government institution. It was a very emotional experience for me to see the very building where I was converted over sixty years ago. The elderly looking security guard would not let us in through the gate until in my pleading I mentioned that I was converted there in 1948. In disbelief, he exclaimed, "I wasn't even born then!"

After breakfast, Israel came to take us to the big meeting, which was mainly the ordination of about twelve pastors, including their wives. The conference had brought together members of the denomination coming from the whole of Kwa-Zulu Natal. I learned there that this was the Norwegian Mission Union, the very small first mission school I had taught at fresh from the ETTC! It had made phenomenal growth after the death of Hageman at Ekuthandaneni near Stanger, just north of Durban. Hageman was the head of that mission station.

The president of this denomination, now called the Independent Baptist Church (IBC), was to introduce me. I had casually met him earlier as I was introduced to him.

To my utter amazement, he took about fifteen minutes telling the audience about his professor at Union Bible Institute! He was obviously a quiet, serious and dignified student. At first he seemed like someone I had never met before.

The entire worship service was very powerful. Young couples there for ordination seemed a very dedicated bunch, keen to be used by the Lord in their ministry. I was to preach and challenge them and the congregants prayed for them as they knelt around the altar. After that profoundly blessed service, we drove back to Empangeni.

The reception given to us by our grandchildren and great-grandchildren was humbling. Many of them knew me by name. They all met Emlinah for the first time. They thoroughly enjoyed their "Gogo" as much as Gogo enjoyed them. We visited homes of a number of those living in the city. But the final gathering was at Israel's home. The house was packed, and it was like a church service. They sang Christian songs passionately at the top of their lungs, and some gave their testimonies, others introducing their kids and how they were doing at school and at work. One of Israel's sons has founded a ministry. He is an evangelist and showed us the website he had created. It was really something to witness that kind of enthusiasm!

BACK TO KWA-MASHU

From Empangeni, Israel took us back to Kwa-Mashu where the trip started in November. Our beloved Pastor Adromat had arranged that we would spend Christmas with her so that from there we would fly to Johannesburg to catch our flight back home. Israel, with his wife, Ntombifuthi, drove us to Durban. We spent the remaining days trying to find Emlinah's Permanent Resident card, which was promised to be in our hands within thirty days. Dozens of calls yielded no result. As one point I personally spoke to officials at Pearson Airport in Toronto. We finally agreed that she would get the PR card at the airport and we would find it waiting for us there.

That never happened. Somehow, Sibusiso convinced the lady at check-in counter in Durban that we would find the card waiting for us in Toronto. So, we flew to Johannesburg. We spent the whole day at Tambo Airport waiting for the midnight flight to Amsterdam. The airport where we waited was the busiest airport. Passengers were picked up by porters and delivered to their boarding gates ever so frequently. One porter noticed that we had been sitting there for virtually the whole day and he asked us about our flight. We told him. So, when the time came for his shift to end, he told us that he had voluntarily decided he was going to wait until he took us to our plane. Meanwhile, he went for dinner and came back when the Amsterdam flight passengers were called to their boarding gate.

He personally loaded our hand luggage because our six suitcases had been checked in to Toronto, and he took us to our gate. He waited until the plane's departure. He was with us when the gentleman at the boarding gate told us that Emlinah could *not* board that flight. After hearing all our sensible explanations, he reluctantly took us to his lady supervisor. She eventually gathered from Emlinah that we were missionaries. They ordered our luggage out of the plane!

The porter prepared by the Lord for us played a major role in the mess, confusion, and dilemma that ensued, to say the least! The doors of the plane were closed, leaving us in an empty airport. There was no phone. My cell phone was never used on our trip. Not even cleaners were in sight at the airport. Everyone had vanished into thin air except this man who had not been even invited to do this. He would have to find a taxi to get him to his home because there would be no public transport at midnight.

The "Lord's messenger" found us an open gate that would be closing shortly. He hurried us to that area, carrying with us the pile of luggage. This revealed skills that I did not know Emlinah had. She was carrying three things simultaneously: two with her hands and balancing one on her head! The messenger found the lady who was about to lock up and he asked her to phone a local owner of a bed and breakfast hotel situated near the airport. Sure enough, the eighty-eight-year-old lady showed up. She was about four feet tall. No walker and no cane. She brought her driver, who carried all our stuff to her beautiful B and B called The Dove's Nest. This was one day on our trip that looked like a movie! Events like this make you pinch yourself to check if it's a dream or reality. The old lady had a full staff running her business efficiently. They called her "Granny." She was known to the highest management of the airport and related to them directly as you will see later.

We spent the seventh week in Granny's B and B, going through the advice given to us by the supervisor at the Johannesburg airport. Incidentally, she was a Christian and had us in her mind throughout the week. She was the first to recognize us when we came to board the plane back home. We followed her advice as carefully as we could. We made the phone calls to Pretoria and spoke to a person whose name she had given us. When we were ready to get to Pretoria, we spoke to Granny wondering if she might organize some dependable taxi owner she knew to take us there and back. She said, "No, I will take you there myself with a driver I know. You can pay him R500 [CD$50] and I will take you to the Canadian Embassy door and they will help you call this number and I will come and pick you up. Any other taxi driver will drop you off and get another business—you will be left stranded there." The day went as beautifully as Granny had said. Emlinah finally got the Permanent Residence visa stamped in her South African passport. *Hooray!!*

The next day Granny took our tickets and passports to re-book us for our way back home. She went directly to the highest officer to make new bookings for us, where we did not need to join her. Upon her return she told us she had turned down the earliest possible flight. She did not trust it because mechanics were completing work on it. It had some engine trouble. She booked us on a later KLM flight departing at midnight December 31st—the same one we were prevented from boarding the previous week.

The driver took us to the airport. As we settled down after boarding the plane, a lovely Jewish couple with their five lovely children introduced themselves to us. He said that they would have their brief prayer time. We joined them quietly as we did not understand Hebrew. The father, who seemed a very friendly man, was sitting next to me and started talking to us. He knew all about Apartheid in South Africa. When we were fully airborne, the pilot greeted the passengers and said, "Happy New Year."

When loud clapping died down, my talkative wife told our friendly Jewish neighbour, "My husband is a New Year baby." He responded by getting his family to sing loudly, "Happy Birthday!" They were joined by a couple of immediate neighbours. Our trip home went very well from then on.

We have not ceased to marvel at the way the Lord undertook for us all the way. We had very little cash in our pockets when we left Toronto. We could hardly estimate accurately how much money we would need. But we were amazed at the way some people gave us cash all along the way, even where we thought we would need to reimburse them for hospitality. We concluded that many friends and family were continuing to lift us up in prayer. No one could ever plan the kind of unexpected people who contributed so much to meet our needs, especially total strangers.

*"The one who calls you is **faithful**, and he will do it"* (1 Thessalonians 5:24, emphasis added).

www.ingramcontent.com/pod-product-compliance
Lightning Source LLC
Chambersburg PA
CBHW071259280526
45788CB00004B/1774